ENTREPRENEURSHIP

KEY TO SECURING YOUR FUTURE

SOLOMON OKUSIRIKI

DEDICATION

THIS WORK IS DEDICATED TO ALL WHO DESIRE A GREAT FUTURE THROUGH ENTREPRENEURSHIP. TO YOUR SUCCESS

ACKNOWLEDGEMENT

My special thanks go to my wife and children for their support.

I appreciate my colleagues at work for their encouragement.

Most of all, my special thanks goes to the Almighty God for his wisdom and grace that are available to me.

TABLE OF CONTENTS

Introduction   4

Chapter One: Why Entrepreneurship? 6

Chapter Two: Starting a Business While in Paid Employment 9

Chapter Three: Discovering Your Business 15

Chapter Four: Raising Finance for Your Business 24

Chapter Five: Vision; A Key to Business Success 34

Chapter Six: The Place of Diligence 40

INTRODUCTION

Many look to the future with fear and uncertainty in their hearts. A major reason for this fear stems from a lack of preparation for the future. The future is too important to be left to chance. It must be prepared for. To secure a bright and enviable future, one must therefore, prepare for the future.

Preparation is a major key to success in life. When opportunity meets preparation, success is guaranteed.

Sad to say, many don't prepare for the future, they just keep wishing and hoping that the future will be better, but only end up with a horrible future. You must understand that securing a better tomorrow requires much more than wishing and hoping; practical steps must be taken to ensure it.

A careful study of today's employees reveals that only a few actually prepare for the future. The majority live for today and wish for tomorrow. All their earnings are spent on consumables. They don't have any meaningful investment for tomorrow. They give excuses as to the inadequacy of their earnings to meet their needs, let alone setting aside part of the same earnings for investment purposes. As a result, they are made to face the nemesis of their lack of financial plan at retirement, living in abject poverty.

This work aims at preparing you for retirement. It deals with securing your future through **ENTREPRENEURSHIP**.

FELICIA OKUSIRIKI

CHAPTER ONE

WHY ENTREPRENEURSHIP?

On an early cold harmattan morning, I was on my way to the Local Government office to deliver a paper on Entrepreneurship when I saw certain men in their forties and fifties involved in manual labor in the cold. I was troubled for them because this exposure can lead to some serious health challenges apart from the fact that the wages they will be paid will not amount to much. I had to take the task of preparing for my future more seriously because I wouldn't want to be seen in such a situation at that stage of my life.

Entrepreneurship is important for anyone that intends to be successful in life as it is the primary road to wealth creation. It is not for the feeble or for those content to flow with the tide of life. It is for those who are ready to "chance the tide" and take a risk.

Entrepreneurship is the act and process of identifying business opportunities and gathering the necessary resources to initiate a successful business activity. Thus, an entrepreneur is a person who is able to identify a need and subsequently take practical steps to meet the need so identified. He organizes a commercial undertaking involving risks. He initiates, plans, organizes, controls and assumes the risk of a business undertaking. He coordinates other factors of production towards the achievement of profit maximization.

According to a study conducted in the United States and published by Brian Tracy, a well-respected business coach and consultant, 74% of self-made millionaires came from self-owned businesses most of which were built from the scratch by the entrepreneurs themselves. According to him, in the 19th Century, fortunes were built by people like Andrew Carnegie, J. P. Morgan, Jacob Van Astor, Thomas Edison and others through entrepreneurship.

In the 20th Century, especially in the last few years, businesses and fortunes alike have been built by people like Bill Gates, Steve Case, Sam Walton, Rose Perot and Larry Ellison. Each of these persons started from the scratch and built their businesses into enviable heights.

Understand that as an employee, you make more money for your employer than you do for yourself. The *best good* you can do for yourself is to go beyond your job description to learn and understand how that business works. By so doing, you will learn all the necessary principles that will help you when you start your own business.

Furthermore, entrepreneurship offers tremendous opportunities for people by opening doors to greater self-sufficiency, self-esteem, education and growth.

CHAPTER TWO

STARTING A BUSINESS WHILE IN PAID EMPLOYMENT

In preparing for retirement, it is worthwhile and advisable to start a part-time business while in paid employment. It will deliver you from depending solely on your salary and /or wages. In doing this, the following should be considered:

1. Analyze yourself to determine if you have the will to combine working and starting a business. You will be cheating on your employer if you abandon your job for your business. Rather, it is advisable to do your business in your free time without interfering with your paid job.

2. Is there a policy in your workplace that bars employees from engaging in other businesses other than the job you are paid to do? It will be wrong to disobey

your employer. If this is your situation, consider the following:

a. Set aside a sacrificial amount of money from your salary. It may not be enough for your needs, but it is advisable to see it as a seed you are planting for a harvest in the future. This money should then be invested in an investment that is likely to yield returns commensurate with what you would have had if you had invested it in a business yourself.

b. Meanwhile, spend time studying the technical and Management aspects of the business you are interested in. Carefully study the informal business culture that exists in the business arena, the code of conducts which are not openly said but done, and how you will react to them realistically.

3. If no policy exists to bar employees from owning and running businesses, you should first scrutinize your environment for business opportunities that exist in the marketplace which also suits your interest, purpose and personality. Your selected business should have the potential to grow into a major source of living. It should be something that can be done within your home environment and can be left with someone you can trust.

Some of the businesses you can do on a part time basis can be classified under the following sectors:

1. **AGRO ALLIED SECTOR:**
   This has to do with agricultural related businesses. Opportunities for part-time businesses include food processing such as preparation of confectionaries at a micro level (cakes, homemade bread, cashew nuts, etc.), small scale farming

(snail farming, poultry for eggs rearing, fish farming), etc.

2. SERVICES SECTOR

The opportunities under this sector can also be done on a part-time basis during your spare time. This sector will specifically benefit the professionals whose services are demanded by the public with little or no assistance for delivery. Examples are Lawyers (offering legal services), doctors (medical services), Linguists (interpretation of documents in various languages), caterers (offering mobile catering services), among others.

In summary, look at what you can do with the skill you have and from which the public can benefit from at a cost; research and find out what others are offering and price fairly. Then look for a cheaper and faster means of getting news out to your target customers.

3. **MANUFACTURING SECTOR**

Remember that you can only venture into areas you can combine with your work. It is advisable to select an idea that can be started in a customized manner, made for specification to the taste of the individual customer and very cost effective though priced at a premium. A major example in this sector is clothing and accessories (garments, shoes). Others include soap-making, etc.

4. **INFORMATION TECHNOLOGY/TELECOMUNICATION**

Businesses under this sector include call centers, website designs, information gathering, internet centers, business centers, etc.

5. **TOURISM/HOSPITALITY**

This includes event packaging, master of ceremonies, TV viewing centers, tour services, etc.

CHAPTER REFERENCES

1. Angela Itambo (2005). *Starting a Business While in Paid Employment*. Businessday Small Business Journal, July 11, 2005.

CHAPTER THREE

DISCOVERING YOUR BUSINESS

Discovering the right type of business to invest in can be a problem to many. For some, their hobbies can be turned into either a part-time or full time business while others just venture into something else.

Whether one is engaged in a part-time or full-time business, two important things to note include:

- Do you have the skills and/or talent to run a business?
- Is there a market for what you are offering? Are there people willing to buy what you intend to sell?

To find out if you are truly ready to run a business, ask yourself the following questions:

- What do I know about starting and running a business
- What kind of business do I want to start?
- Do I really want to give up my leisure activities (like watching TV, etc.) to run a business?
- Will running a business disturb my studies or official activities in my workplace?
- Will my relations help me out?
- How much money, if any, will it cost to start my business?
- Where will I get the money to buy the supplies or equipment I may need to run my business?

To find out if there is a market for your product(s) and /or service(s), ask yourself the following questions:

- Will people want to buy what I am selling?
- Who will most likely buy what I am selling and why?

- How will people know about my business?
- Will other people be selling the same thing I am selling?
- If other people are selling the same thing, what should I do to differentiate and make my product(s) and/or service(s) preferable by customers?
- What combination of advertisements strategies will I use to get people to buy my product(s)?
- How much will it cost and how often will I need to advertise?
- Where will my business be located?

SELECTING A BUSINESS IDEA

The heart of every great business is the core idea that creates the business. Ideas rule the world. Most successful businesses began with the adoption of an idea. It is advisable that one be cautious when it comes to selecting the idea that would hold the ace to your desire for financial freedom and self-actualization. This is very necessary especially in a business climate like ours. The reason so many people are dissuaded from starting businesses is the tale of woes perpetuated by those that have gotten their fingers burnt in business.

Your desire to choose a business idea should not be motivated by any of the following:

- Having a particular business in mind should not be born out of a current hype in a business idea
- Choosing a business idea should not be because a friend or colleague made a huge sum of money from it, and you have what it takes to do the same

At no time should your decision to start a business be motivated by any of the above. Often, such businesses are short-lived.

Where then, do great business ideas come from?

They come from your personal experiences, encounters, hobbies and interests. They come from your work-related experiences e.g. working in restaurants, cyber cafes, computer centers, stores, etc.

What makes a great business idea?

- the idea is concrete
- it is feasible
- it identifies a market need

Talking about identifying a need, it is actually the cornerstone on which a successful business rests. Your most important objective should not be to make money, even though it is a very important factor in owning a business. It should be to add value, to solve a problem for someone. Look around to identify the problems people want so desperately solved.

When you identify your own needs, it becomes easier to identify the needs of others because other people are just like you. As you decide to meet these needs, you'll find yourself in business.

Furthermore, to select a suitable business idea, you must be prepared to first embark on a thorough self-analysis of your personality, what weakness exists and how you can address them.

Also, be aware that not all business idea promoted by the government or consultants is meant for you. You must identify what will work for you and have in mind that the business idea you choose –

- must be able to sustain itself without needing further cash injection after some time except for expansion purposes,
- can be started small,
- Should have a diversified customer base. This ensures your business is not just

dependent on a single customer base so that the closure of that consumer base will not mean the end of your business,

- Should, with time, have the ability to attract competent staff,
- Should never be at the expense of your family, community and your health.

You must understand that going into business is about serving people with what you have, therefore, a lot of intelligence must be embarked upon to know about the marketing environment and how to search for unmet ideas.

To have this intelligence, it is advised that the following be done:

- Be motivated and determined to spot developments in the environment.
- Find out from distributors and retailers especially within your locality on suggested starting point.

- Take time to study carefully various opportunities, no matter how profitable they appear on paper. Then, weigh such opportunities alongside the threats attached to it, in terms of current government policies and likely future actions. This can be achieved by closely following the news on agitations from different interest groups, latest happenings in the global market and conditions and modalities set by regulatory bodies, both domestically and internationally.

CHAPTER REFERENCES

1. *Businessday* Small Business Journal, Monday April 25, 2005; *"How to Start a Business"*

2. Angela Itambo (2005). *Becoming an Entrepreneur.* Businessday Small Business Journal, Monday May 9th, 2005.

3. Angela Itambo (2005). *Selecting a Suitable Business Idea.* Businessday Small Business Journal, Monday June 27th, 2005.

4. Sam Adeyemi (2005). *Own A Business.* Thisday Saturday Newspaper, July 9, 2005. Vol. 11, No. 3730.

CHAPTER FOUR

RAISING FINANCE FOR YOUR BUSINESS

Based on your research, you have selected a suitable business idea and written the business plan. The next step therefore, is how to raise the funds required to kick start the business.

An initial research will help you identify possible financiers that could be approached.

Also, your business plan would have revealed how much you need and what you need the money for. Getting the money you need for your business as and at when required breathes life into your business and gives it a forward momentum that propels it forward. Therefore, to improve your chances of getting the money you need, some fundamental finance issues should be understood.

Finding money is just a matter of being informed and choosing the right path for money to enter the business.

There are several options available to you while searching for financing. Some methods for raising funds are less difficult than others, but all require some planning. The process of getting finance requires that you know the answers to the following basic questions:

- **Do you really need the money?**
  It is important to ask and answer this question with all honesty. At times, after careful introspection most entrepreneurs discover that the need for money was not as pressing as it initially appeared. They discover that they can manage the existing cash flow more effectively.

- **How do you define your need?**
  Accurately defining your need brings clarity and focus to the finance sourcing

process and helps in turn to channel your energy in the right direction. The basic questions here are: is the money needed for expansion, or is it needed to cushion against risks?

- **What will you use the money for?**
  You must know exactly where the money will be used. You must be specific because generalities are recipes for disaster. Carefully identify the areas from where money should flow into your business.

- **How much money do you need?**
  You should calculate how much will carry you through initial start-up and into the first several months of operation. It is Imperative to have a realistic picture of your needs. This is not about being a pessimist or an optimist; many businesses have failed because the

money ran out before the business reached profitability.

- **How will you pay back the money?**
You must have adequate cash flow from your business to repay the money to your source. Before requesting for funds, make sure your fiscal projections and business integrity are soundly argued in a good business plan. You need to show sufficient cash flow in your business for repayment. You do this with information as found in an income statement, a Statement of Affairs, and a projected cash flow statement.

- **How does your need for financing align with your business plan?**
Integral parts of a good business plan are financial statements for your business. A good business plan gets you focused and forces you to articulate your vision, demonstrates your seriousness,

and most importantly, when shopping for funds, comes in handy as a marketing tool. It is therefore, imperative that the need for funds is in tandem with the terms contained in the business plan.

WHERE TO SOURCE FOR FUNDS

- **Private Sources**
These consist of your personal savings, friends and families.

The easiest and most stress-free source of finance is your personal savings. No one asks you questions, and you are not accountable to anyone but yourself. This is assuming you have saved up some money before venturing out to set up your own business. If your savings are low, put off that vacation, drive your old car a bit longer, avoid large purchases-be thrifty in all areas and you can save faster for your business. Know that most lenders won't finance 100 percent of your business, so you will need to invest some money yourself. Showing that you are willing to take a personal risk yourself will encourage financiers to want to take a risk with you.

Also, borrowing from your friends and family is a good way for new businesses to get money. The advantages are numerous. In most cases, the fund is cheap, since there are no finance charges. It is not uncommon for relatives to make low interest or no interest loans to family members.

Private sources save you the hassles of searching for funds, and the time consumed in the process could be channeled towards other productive purposes.

The flip-side however, is that you lose interest you could have earned on your money, in addition to the cushion savings provide for any future emergencies.

Also, potential problems arise with friends and family if the business falls on hard times and you have trouble repaying the loan. It is always advisable to make sure all parties are aware of the risks involved before making the decision to lend the money.

- **The Bank**

The bank is the most popular source of finance that comes to most people's minds. In case you choose to go along the line or to other external funding organizations, it is imperative that your business plan is sound. Sound, meaning it is well written, clearly defines the business idea, and displays great potential and return on investment. In other words, your business plan is your written sales pitch towards convincing an investor to lend you money or invest in your business. Ensure you have and maintain a healthy relationship with the bank, a guarantor who is willing to stand for you or assets as collateral. You could either apply for a loan or request an overdraft. The loan could be a short term or long term business loan. Ensure you compare the interest rates and repayment terms offered by various banks.

The disadvantage here is that most banks endeavor to reduce the risk they are exposed to in granting loans by offering the service to a select group of established companies with proven track records. The loans also come at a cost in the form of finance charges and interests, and in the event that the business does not do well you risk losing your assets.

- **Venture Capitals**

  These are institutional risk takers, groups of wealthy individuals, government assisted sources or major financial institutions. Venture capitalists are the most common source of professional equity funding, and they mostly prefer three to five year old companies that have the potential to return higher than average profits.

You might want to consider soliciting professional help when looking to raise large sums of fund for the business.

All in all, before investing the funds into the business ensure you follow the financial plan as contained in your business plan.

CHAPTER REFERENCES

1. Yvonne Ruke Akpoveta (2005). *Raising Finance for the Business.* Businessday Small Business Journal, Monday April 4, 2005.

2. Fate Link Column (2005). *How to Source Money for your Business(1).* Businessday Small Business Journal, Monday May 9, 2005,

CHAPTER FIVE

VISION; A KEY TO BUSINESS SUCCESS

Business success can be attained and sustained if you have a clear vision for the business. The vision you have for your business is what will propel you to do things that you would not have done normally.

The man, Bill Gates became the richest man on earth in 1995 and remained there for a very long time. It is a common saying that it is easy to make it to the top but very difficult to remain on top. Therefore, what could have been responsible for keeping this man as the world's richest man for a long time?

Despite the competitive environment Bill Gates found himself, he was still ahead. One thing made this extraordinary human being to stand out. That thing is vision.

Bill Gates started out with a very powerful vision. He wanted a world where there will be a

Personal Computer (PC) in every home and every office. That was a tall vision back in 1975 when Microsoft was started and only a few companies had computers.

Today the situation is different. Computers are all over the place. Microsoft is creating so much of sophisticated and fine software packages meant to simplify computing tasks every now and then.

Microsoft quickly jumped on the internet bandwagon to be able to deliver on its vision. The constant improvement in the computer world is making more people to continue buying and buying. Once a new version of Microsoft Windows comes out nobody wants to use the old version again since the new version would offer remarkable improvements on the previous one. With this strategy, it is difficult for Microsoft Windows to lack patronage.

The vision of a computer in every home is yet to be delivered worldwide today. That explains why Bill Gates refused to take any rest. The only time he withdraws from work is the three weeks of heavy intellectual work which he calls thinking weeks. That is a time he does not see anybody, even his wife. All he does is just think, think and think. This is how tenacious this great man is to the fulfilment of his vision.

Bill Gates actually resigned as CEO of Microsoft in year 2000 to become the Chief Software Architect of the company in order to concentrate on the core function that drives the growth of the company.

This guy is so much driven by his vision that the money Microsoft makes is not even of much interest to him. He is so much consumed by the vision that he is not even interested in the comfort of the CEO's office. He left that to his childhood friend and partner, Steve Ballmer.

Though retired official today, he took on a new post as Technology Adviser to support the current CEO of Microsoft.

I don't know if you have a vision for your business. I don't know if that vision is clear for everyone to see. I don't know how consumed you are with the vision. I don't know if temporary financial success has caused you to abandon what you set out to achieve and you are now laid back to enjoy the success. Vision is the driver of success and when vision goes to sleep, success heads for a crash.

Vision is fueled by the passion put into the pursuit of same vision. If you are passionate in the pursuit of the vision you have per time, you will see greater and more powerful dimensions of same vision unfolding before you.

Understand that every vision is realizable. Every business dream you have can be actualized. Dream crazy dreams. The crazier the better because that is what changes the world.

When Bill Gates was dreaming about a computer in every home, most computers at that time were housed in large halls and required serious air-conditioning because of the heat they generated. Today, we have gadgets like palm tops (hand held computer devices) that perform the same tasks. Crazy things are now being done with computers today because these guys continue to dream crazy dreams.

CHAPTER REFERENCES

1. Businessday Small Business Journal, Monday April 25, 2005; *Bill Gates Worked 5 Days Without a Break (3).*

CHAPTER SIX

THE PLACE OF DILIGENCE

From the previous chapter, it is clear that it takes diligence to work out one's vision. According to Thomas Edison, success is one percent inspiration and ninety-nine percent perspiration. No matter how wonderful your vision is, it will make no meaning if you don't set out to work it out.

Inspiration is so immaterial on the scale of somebody like Thomas Edison that he allocated one percent to it. This means that if Thomas Edison were to be a university lecturer and you brought a unique idea to him (no matter how revolutionary it appears), you can never score more than one percent. Tell him you are going to make a car that will fly from one planet to another. Tell him you are going to put up a skyscraper that will reach the heavens. Tell him your revolutionary aircraft will take off from your rooftop and fly round the world and land back on your rooftop without stopping to refuel. Tell him you will make cars run on water instead of gasoline. I bet you, the man will just take your script and give you just one percent without a second thought.

Why won't he? He went through the experience himself. So many experts had tried inventing the incandescent bulb before him. The only lamp existing at that time was no better than a few candles put together.

So many had the flash of inspiration that it was possible to have a lamp that will be bright enough to lighten the house just like the light of the day without generating too much heat and which the electricity supply at that time could power. So many possessed the idea, meaning it was not Edison's original idea. It was brought to him. Somebody had challenged him to work on it since they knew his record of previous revolutionary inventions. He had recorded so many improvements on the telegraph and countless others. However, the incandescent bulb challenge presented a daunting opportunity to him. It appeared exciting and so he jumped into it and confronted the task casually at first but soon discovered that it was not going to be like the previous inventions.

He continued trying his best. Each new trial met with failure. At a particular time, he experimented with about 160 metals passing each through hundreds of tests. The first challenge was to get a metal strong enough to allow electricity to pass through it without burning off and light enough in terms of its weight to produce light when the electricity passes through. The series of tests produced failure after failure. He thought he got near to the answer once and invited industry giants for a demonstration. The filament burnt off after a few seconds in front of a huge crowd. What a huge failure and a big shame. He was even branded a charlatan. However, he refused to be deterred.

He went back to his laboratory and continued his experiments. He started with another round of metals. He finally arrived at the answer with carbon. Thereafter, he moved to the next challenge. This was to depressurize the bulb's atmosphere so that the glow of the light could be bright and sustained. The vacuum created in the bulb must be perfected. It took the form of pumping air out of the bulb using all kind of means. That expedition demanded hundreds of tests too.

At the end of the day, he was able to shout eureka when he finally perfected the invention. We might still have been using the kerosene lamp up till today if not for the diligence of Thomas Edison because nobody else would have been able to go through that kind of pain and stress to achieve an objective.

This is why I feel sorry for those who bandy so many ideas about and announce to everyone how their ideas will change the world and they end up not lifting a finger.

I want you to be comfortable with only one flash of inspiration. That is enough to feed you for life. The next thing you need to do with that flash of inspiration (that revolutionary idea you have) is to roll up your sleeves and get down to serious work. You just have to work on your idea if it must work. Work is a sure way to success particularly if what you want is business success. Show me any successful business person and I will show you somebody who values the virtue of hard work.

You may ask, how do I work to make my idea or business work? I will quickly answer that you sit down and begin to take practical steps to actualize whatever business idea you have. You may want to try out a new procedure or process in your business or start selling in a new territory. Just stand up and take steps in the direction of your goal. Don't be discouraged by initial attempts that ended up in failure. Just like Thomas Edison, regard your initial failures as ways in which the idea will not work and so eliminating the possibility of using those strategies again in future.

It is now easy to make bulbs because people do not have to try the various ways Thomas Edison had tried and which ended in failure.

Mention any successful business person around and I will not hesitate to tell you he must be a hard working fellow.

If you are ready to perspire and persist on your business idea the way Thomas Edison did, you will still break the success barrier.

Stay on the business idea and work on it like a hen will sit on its eggs until they hatch. That business must hatch success for you.

CHAPTER REFERENCES

1. Kola Owolabi (2005). Businessday Small Business Journal, June 27, 2005. Vol. 4 No.091.